For Katie Cunningham

BECOMING BABE RUTH

MATT TAVARES

Candlewick Press

Baltimore, 1902

George Ruth lives with his parents
and his baby sister
in a tiny apartment above a saloon.

Most days, he skips school
and roams the streets.
He steals tomatoes from a vegetable stand
and throws them at passing wagons.
He sneaks into the saloon
and takes money from the register.

Finally, when he is seven years old,
his parents decide enough is enough.

On June 13, 1902,
George stands with his father
outside Saint Mary's
Industrial School for Boys.
Tears well up in George's eyes.
He squeezes his father's hand
and begs him for one more chance.

But it's too late.

Saint Mary's is a school, not a prison.
But the eight hundred boys who live there
call themselves inmates.
Every day, the inmates wake up
at six o'clock sharp.
They wash, get dressed, go to church,
then hurry to the cafeteria.

They eat breakfast in complete silence.
If they talk, they might get whipped.
They eat the same food every day.

They go to class.
They go to work.
They follow the rules.

George does not like following rules,
and he does not like going to class.
He misses his parents
and his baby sister.

But there is one thing that
he does like about Saint Mary's.

Almost every day,
after all his work is done,
George gets to play baseball.

One cloudy afternoon,
George is playing ball in the Little Yard,
where the younger kids play,
when someone in the Big Yard shouts,
"Brother Matthias is going to hit!"

The game stops.
George grabs his glove
and runs after the other boys.

Brother Matthias
jogs past the crowd
with quick, pigeon-toed strides.
He stands at home plate
and tosses a baseball into the air.
Then, holding the bat with just one hand,
he takes a gigantic upper-cut swing
that sends the ball soaring
high above the Big Yard,
over the outfield,
beyond the trees.

He repeats this magnificent act
again and again.

George pushes his way to the front.
He has never seen anything like it.

Years pass, and after a while
Saint Mary's starts to feel like home.
George has lots of friends.
He works in the tailor shop and
becomes an expert shirtmaker.
He plays in two hundred ball games a year,
even in winter. Even when he has to
shovel snow off the base paths.

Brother Matthias spends countless hours
teaching George how to throw a curveball,
how to turn a double play,
how to pick off a runner at first.
George learns how to play
catcher, shortstop, and
every other position on the field.
He practices and practices.

By the time he is sixteen,
George is the biggest,
strongest boy at Saint Mary's—
and the best ballplayer, too.
He strolls toward the plate.
The pitcher whirls around.
"BACK UP!" he yells to his outfielders.
They are already running.
Someone in the outfield yells,
"George is going to hit!"
The younger boys run
from the Little Yard to watch.

The pitcher winds up.
George takes a gigantic upper-cut swing
and sends the ball soaring
high above the Big Yard,
way over the outfield,
beyond the trees.
The boys watch in amazement.
George circles the bases
with quick, pigeon-toed strides.

One day, George hits three home runs in a game.
Another day, he strikes out twenty-two batters.
As soon as the game ends,
still in his baseball uniform,
he joins the school band in the bleachers
and pounds away on a big bass drum.

Crowds of people come to watch him play.
They tell their friends about him,
and their friends tell their friends.
Soon, word spreads all the way to Jack Dunn,
the owner of the minor-league Baltimore Orioles.

On February 14, 1914,
Mr. Dunn goes to Saint Mary's
and watches George pitch for thirty minutes.
He offers him a contract right then and there.

Two weeks later,
George says good-bye to his friends.
Brother Matthias shakes his hand.
"You'll make it, George," he says.
He opens the gate,
and George walks out.

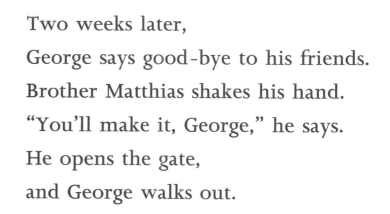

Outside the gate, everything is new.
George gets to ride on a train!
He gets to stay in a hotel!
He gets to eat dinner at a restaurant!

"Where'd they get *this* kid?"
one of his new teammates asks.
"He's one of Jack Dunn's new babes,"
another teammate replies.
After that, they all start calling him Babe.

Soon even the newspapers are
calling George by his new name:
Babe Ruth.

The season starts, and Babe Ruth
is one of the Orioles' best pitchers.
Some days, he plays for
the Orioles in the afternoon,
then rides his bike to Saint Mary's
and spends the evening
playing ball with his friends.

He plays so well
that halfway into the season,
the Orioles sell his contract
to the Boston Red Sox.

On July 10, 1914,
he boards a northbound train
on his way to the major leagues.

Before long, Babe Ruth
is the best pitcher in baseball.
In 1916, he leads the league
with a 1.75 earned run average.
In 1917, he wins twenty-four games.
His team wins the World Series
three times, in 1915, 1916, and 1918.

In 1919, the Red Sox switch
Babe Ruth to the outfield,
to keep his powerful bat
in the lineup every day.
With his grand upper-cut swing,
he launches home run after home run
high into the right-field bleachers.

Back at St. Mary's, Brother Matthias
and the boys read about him
in the newspaper every day.

On January 5, 1920,
they are shocked by the front-page news:
Babe Ruth has been sold
to the New York Yankees for
one hundred twenty-five thousand dollars—
the largest sum any team has ever paid
for a baseball player.

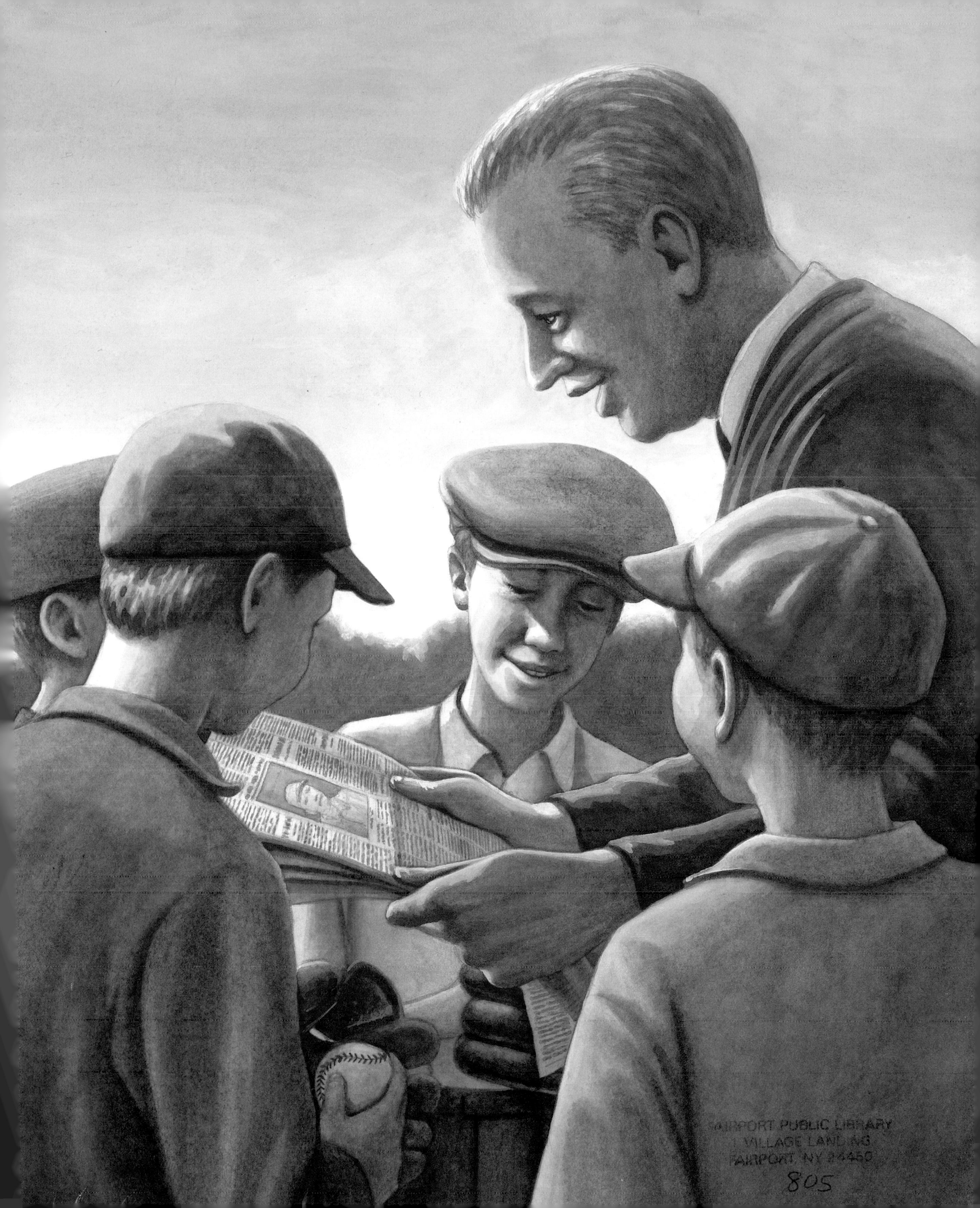

Babe Ruth arrives in New York City
in the spring of 1920 and
quickly becomes the biggest celebrity
in the biggest city in America.
A flock of newspaper writers
follows him everywhere he goes.

He wears fancy clothes,
custom tailored just for him.
He drives fast cars
and throws wild parties.
He eats enormous amounts of food.
He does whatever he wants.

And he clobbers the baseball
like nobody ever has.
Halfway into his first season
as a New York Yankee,
he has already broken baseball's
single-season home-run record.

All across America,
baseball fans are mesmerized.
They have never seen anything like it.
Everywhere he goes,
people cheer for him.
Newspaper writers make up
new nicknames for him:
"The Batterer," "The Colossus,"
and "The Sultan of Swat."

But there is bad news from Baltimore.

A fire has swept through
Saint Mary's Industrial School for Boys.
Nearly every building has been destroyed.
Babe Ruth has an idea.
He writes a letter to Brother Matthias.

On September 8, 1920,
Brother Matthias opens the gates
and fifty inmates walk out,
carrying tubas, trumpets, trombones,
and a big bass drum.

For the final two weeks
of the 1920 baseball season,
the school band from Saint Mary's
gets to join the New York Yankees
on a road trip across America.
They get to ride on a train,
as special guests of Babe Ruth.
He invites them all to the dining car
and buys everybody ice cream.

The fifty boys from Saint Mary's
get to go to all the games.
They play a concert in the stands
before each game
and another concert every night.

Babe Ruth is at every show.
Huge crowds attend the concerts,
eager to meet the Babe in person
and happy to donate money
to help rebuild the place where
the "Sultan of Swat"
learned how to play baseball.

Back in New York,
Babe Ruth strolls toward the plate.
He sees Brother Matthias
sitting in the grandstand
with the boys from Saint Mary's.
He waves and tips his cap.
The boys' faces beam with pride.

Years later,
Brother Matthias is playing ball
with a group of boys
in the Little Yard,
outside the newly rebuilt dormitory.
Someone in the outfield yells,
"HE'S HERE!"

The game stops,
and all the boys run to the Big Yard
as fast as they can.

George tosses a baseball up in the air
and takes a gigantic upper-cut swing
that sends the ball soaring
high above the Big Yard,
past the outfield,
beyond the trees.

The boys cheer with delight
as he repeats this magnificent act
again and again.

Author's Note

There was no television in the 1920s, no nightly Babe Ruth highlight reel for fans to watch with their own eyes. Other than grainy black-and-white footage on newsreels at movie theaters, and occasional big games broadcast on the radio, fans of Babe Ruth either saw him in person at the ballpark or read about him in the newspaper.

Dozens of writers earned their living by describing his daily exploits in vivid detail, from his magnificent home runs to his enormous dinners. The newspapers provided the amazing stories, along with a steady stream of black-and-white photographs of his unforgettable face. The rest was left to the imaginations of millions, where the legend of Babe Ruth grew to mythic proportions.

He became a symbol of everything big, loud, and powerful in America during the Roaring Twenties. And to the boys at Saint Mary's, and to children living in reform schools and orphanages all across America, he was a real-life folk hero, a beacon of hope. He was one of them—a kid from nowhere who made it all the way to the top.

Babe Ruth embraced this role. When the newspapers called him an orphan, he never denied it because he knew it would make orphans happy to think that he was one too. And as he traveled around the country playing baseball, he made countless visits to orphanages, hospitals, and reform schools, talking with the kids, joking around, and signing autographs.

As a lifelong baseball fan, I've always been fascinated by Babe Ruth. As I researched his life, one thing that struck me was the fact that even the "Sultan of Swat," who seemed to possess superhuman abilities, needed lots of help along the way. Becoming the king of baseball took countless hours of practice and plenty of support and guidance from his school and from his teacher and mentor, Brother Matthias. And even at the height of his fame, he remained eternally grateful to those who helped him become Babe Ruth.

The story of Babe Ruth is a true American fairy tale. Sent away to reform school at the age of seven, George Herman Ruth transcended his circumstances and became not only the greatest all-around player in baseball history, but one of the most enduring iconic figures in American history.

GEORGE "BABE" RUTH

Height: 6 feet 2 inches; Weight: 215 lbs.; Born: February 6, 1895, in Baltimore, Maryland

PITCHING STATS

YEAR	TEAM	W	L	ERA	G	CG	SHO	IP	H	HR	BB	SO
1914	Red Sox	2	1	3.91	4	1	0	23.0	21	1	7	3
1915	Red Sox	18	8	2.44	32	16	1	217.2	166	3	85	112
1916	Red Sox	23	12	**1.75**	44	23	**9**	323.2	230	0	118	170
1917	Red Sox	24	13	2.01	41	**35**	6	326.1	244	2	108	128
1918	Red Sox	13	7	2.22	20	18	1	166.1	125	1	49	40
1919	Red Sox	9	5	2.97	17	12	0	133.1	148	2	58	30
1920	Yankees	1	0	4.50	1	0	0	4.0	3	0	2	0
1921	Yankees	2	0	9.00	2	0	0	9.0	14	1	9	2
1930	Yankees	1	0	3.00	1	1	0	9.0	11	0	2	3
1933	Yankees	1	0	5.00	1	1	0	9.0	12	0	3	0
Career		94	46	2.28	163	107	17	1221.1	974	10	441	488

Key for pitching stats: W = Wins, L = Losses, ERA = Earned Run Average, G = Games Played, CG = Complete Games, SHO = Shutouts, IP = Innings Pitched, H = Hits Allowed, HR = Home Runs Allowed, BB = Walks Allowed, SO = Strikeouts. Bold stats represent instances where Babe Ruth led the league.

HITTING STATS

YEAR	TEAM	G	AB	R	H	HR	RBI	BB	BA	OBP	SLG	TB
1914	Red Sox	5	10	1	2	0	2	0	.200	.200	.300	3
1915	Red Sox	42	92	16	29	4	21	9	.315	.376	.576	53
1916	Red Sox	67	136	18	37	3	15	10	.272	.322	.419	57
1917	Red Sox	52	123	14	40	2	12	12	.325	.385	.472	58
1918	Red Sox	95	317	50	95	**11**	66	58	.300	.411	**.555**	176
1919	Red Sox	130	432	**103**	139	**29**	**114**	101	.322	**.456**	**.657**	**284**
1920	Yankees	142	458	**158**	172	**54**	**137**	**150**	.376	**.532**	**.847**	388
1921	Yankees	152	540	**177**	204	**59**	**171**	145	.378	**.512**	**.846**	**457**
1922	Yankees	110	406	94	128	35	99	84	.315	.434	**.672**	273
1923	Yankees	152	522	**151**	205	**41**	131	**170**	.393	**.545**	**.764**	**399**
1924	Yankees	153	529	**143**	200	**46**	121	**142**	**.378**	**.513**	**.739**	**391**
1925	Yankees	98	359	61	104	25	66	59	.290	.393	.543	195
1926	Yankees	152	495	**139**	184	**47**	**146**	**144**	.372	**.516**	**.737**	**365**
1927	Yankees	151	540	**158**	192	**60**	164	137	.356	**.486**	**.772**	417
1928	Yankees	154	536	**163**	173	**54**	**142**	137	.323	.463	**.709**	**380**
1929	Yankees	135	499	121	172	**46**	154	72	.345	.430	**.697**	348
1930	Yankees	145	518	150	186	**49**	153	**136**	.359	**.493**	**.732**	379
1931	Yankees	145	534	149	199	**46**	163	**128**	.373	**.495**	**.700**	374
1932	Yankees	133	457	120	156	41	137	**130**	.341	**.489**	.661	302
1933	Yankees	137	459	97	138	34	103	**114**	.301	.442	.582	267
1934	Yankees	125	365	78	105	22	84	104	.288	.448	.537	196
1935	Braves	28	72	13	13	6	12	20	.181	.359	.431	31
Career		2503	8399	2174	2873	714	2213	2062	.342	.474	.690	5793

Key for hitting stats: G = Games, AB = At Bats, R = Runs, H = Hits, HR = Home Runs, RBI = Runs Batted In, BB = Walks, BA = Batting Average, OBP = On Base Percentage, SLG = Slugging Percentage, TB = Total Bases. Bold stats represent instances where Babe Ruth led the league.

Bibliography

Creamer, Robert W. *Babe: The Legend Comes to Life.* New York: Simon and Schuster, 1974.

Gilbert, Brother C.F.X. *Young Babe Ruth: His Early Life and Baseball Career, from the Memoirs of a Xaverian Brother.* Edited by Harry Rothgerber. Jefferson, NC: McFarland, 1999.

Montville, Leigh. *The Big Bam: The Life and Times of Babe Ruth.* New York: Doubleday, 2006.

Ruth, Babe. *Playing the Game: My Early Years in Baseball.* Edited by William R. Cobb. Mineola, NY: Dover Publications, 2011.

Ruth, George Herman. *Babe Ruth's Own Book of Baseball.* New York: Putnam, 1928.

Smelser, Marshall. *The Life That Ruth Built: A Biography.* New York: Quadrangle/New York Times Book Co., 1975.

Wagenheim, Kal. *Babe Ruth: His Life and Legend.* New York: Praeger, 1974.

Ward, Geoffrey C., and Ken Burns. *Baseball: An Illustrated History.* New York: Knopf, 1994.